WEATHER WATCH

Snow

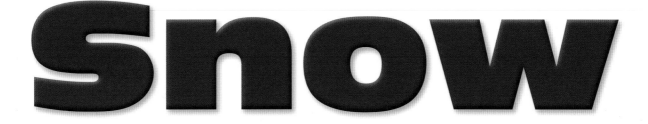

by Alice K. Flanagan

Snowflakes drift down from the sky. They land and collect on the ground. What a pretty sight!

Snow falls in a park.

Snow is frozen **moisture**. But how does snow form? Tiny drops of water in the air gather together and form clouds.

Winter clouds form in the sky.

When it is cold, the drops of water turn into **ice crystals**. These crystals become too heavy to stay in the air. Then they fall as snowflakes.

The first snowfall of the winter covers the ground.

All snowflakes are not the same size. Most are about the size of a pencil eraser. But some can be bigger than a quarter.

Snowflakes come in many shapes and sizes.

Most snowflakes have six sides. No two snowflakes look the same. Snow is clear, too. It just looks white because of the way the light hits it.

Snow falls in a forest.

Snow falls mostly in the winter when it is cold. Some places in the world do not get snow at all. The weather there is too hot for ice crystals to form.

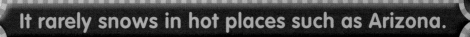
It rarely snows in hot places such as Arizona.

Snow acts like a blanket for the ground. It keeps plant roots safe from the wind and the cold. Snow keeps **burrowing** animals warm and dry.

A gopher stays warm by burrowing under snow.

Sometimes a snowfall can turn into a storm. It is called a **blizzard**.

Snow from a blizzard covers cars on a street.

When snow melts, it fills rivers and lakes. Animals and people can then use the water.

Melting snow drips into a river.

Snow can be light and fluffy or wet and sticky. Have fun when you play in the snow!

A boy and a girl play in the snow.

Glossary

blizzard (BLIZ-urd): A blizzard is a big snowstorm. A blizzard brings lots of snow.

burrowing (BUR-oh-ing): Burrowing means something is digging a hole in the ground to live. Burrowing animals stay warm under snow.

ice crystals (EYESS KRISS-tuls): Ice crystals are water that freezes in certain shapes. Ice crystals can form in clouds.

moisture (MOYS-chur): Moisture is a small amount of water. Frozen moisture forms snow.

To Find Out More

Books

Bauer, Marion Dane. *Snow*. New York: Simon & Schuster, 2003.

Fisher, Carolyn. *The Snow Show*. Orlando, FL: Harcourt, 2008.

Rylant, Cynthia. *Snow*. Orlando, FL: Harcourt, 2008.

Web Sites

Visit our Web site for links about snow:
childsworld.com/links

Note to Parents, Teachers, and Librarians: We routinely verify our Web links to make sure they are safe and active sites. So encourage your readers to check them out!

Index

About the Author

Alice K. Flanagan taught elementary school for ten years. She has been writing for more than twenty years. She has written biographies and books about holidays, careers, animals, and weather.

On the cover: Snow blows off branches in winter.

Published by The Child's World®
1980 Lookout Drive • Mankato, MN 56003-1705
800-599-READ • www.childsworld.com

ACKNOWLEDGMENTS
The Child's World®: Mary Berendes, Publishing Director
The Design Lab: Design and production
Red Line Editorial: Editorial direction

PHOTO CREDITS: Stanislav Pobytov/iStockphoto, cover; iStockphoto, cover, 7, 9, 15; Sven Klaschik/iStockphoto, 3; Peeter Viisimaa/iStockphoto, 5; Adam Gryko/iStockphoto, 11; Alexey Stiop/iStockphoto, 13; Nicholas Belton/iStockphoto, 17; Andrew Penner/iStockphoto, 19; George M. Muresan/iStockphoto, 21

Printed in the United States of America in Mankato, Minnesota.
November 2009
F11460

LIBRARY OF CONGRESS CATALOGING-IN-PUBLICATION DATA
Flanagan, Alice K.
  Snow / Alice K. Flanagan.
    p. cm. — (Weather watch)
  Includes index.
  ISBN 978-1-60253-362-2 (library bound : alk. paper)
  1. Snow—Juvenile literature. I. Title. II. Series.
  QC926.37.F55 2010
  551.57'84—dc22   2009030217